10 SHORTCUTS
Into Our
Prospects' Minds

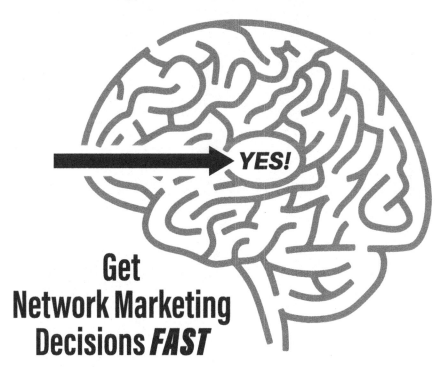

YES!

Get
Network Marketing
Decisions *FAST*

KEITH & TOM "BIG AL" SCHREITER

10 Shortcuts Into Our Prospects' Minds

© 2019 by Keith & Tom "Big Al" Schreiter

Published by Fortune Network Publishing

PO Box 890084

Houston, TX 77289 USA

Telephone: +1 (281) 280-9800

BigAlBooks.com

ISBN-13: 978-1-948197-48-9

CONTENTS

BIG AL
WORKSHOPS

I travel the world 240+ days each year.
Let me know if you want me to stop in your
area and conduct a live Big Al training.

BigAlSeminars.com

FREE Big Al Training Audios
Magic Words for Prospecting
plus Free eBook and the Big Al Report!

BigAlBooks.com/free

PREFACE

Do we know how the human brain works?

Not entirely. But we have general guidelines.

These guidelines help us connect with our prospects at a higher level. When we understand that others have biases, irrational prejudices, and blind spots, we can communicate more effectively.

Do we have to be neuroscientists? Brain researchers? No. We don't even have to be experts on the biology of the brain. Fortunately, scientists pioneered the path and shared their discoveries with us.

This book takes some of those discoveries and puts them into practical applications for our network marketing business.

So what is our mission as network marketers?

Our mission is to get "yes" decisions from our prospects. Our companies do everything else. They don't ask us to come into the home office and handle customer service. We don't design their websites. We don't work in the mail room or the receiving department. In fact, we are not part of the business.

Instead, we partner with the company. They do everything else, and we get "yes" decisions. Seems like a fair deal.

Well, if our job is to get "yes" decisions, now is a good time to learn how to get these decisions. Our first and only stop? The brain.

Prospects make decisions in their brains, not in their feet. Their decisions don't come from the food they eat, magic crystals, or the vibrations of the universe. Yes, their brains make their decisions.

Now, this brings up an interesting question.

"How do our brains work?"

In this book we will take a look at one way to understand our minds. But remember, it is only one viewpoint, not the only viewpoint. Relax. This is not a biology or psychology textbook. Instead, this book is meant to help us have more empathy for our prospects.

We choose this viewpoint because it helps us understand how our prospects make great decisions ... and awful decisions. Then, we can do something about this decision-making process. We won't feel like powerless victims, subject to the whims of prospects' decisions.

IT TOOK 3 TRANQUILIZER DARTS AND A TASER GUN TO BRING HIM DOWN.

Everything was going wrong.

This was the worst opportunity meeting ever.

The amphetamine-crazed speaker talked too fast. Even if the prospects were interested, they couldn't keep up. Too much information in too little time. One long monologue blur.

Was there a connection? No. Everyone felt like the speaker was preaching to them. No engagement. No rapport.

Facts, facts, benefits, more benefits, research quotes, proof, test reports, statistics ... the tsunami didn't end. The only relief came from the company video which prompted everyone to sigh, check their messages, and take a nap.

Could it get worse? Of course. Some nightmares never end.

The high-pressure closing techniques came in waves. Shame, humiliation, and attacks on the prospects' ability to take charge of their lives. Even the distributors felt uncomfortable.

Thankfully, it seemed like the meeting was ending, but no! The speaker guaranteed the disaster by saying, "Oh wait, I forgot. There is more." It took three tranquilizer darts and a taser gun to bring the speaker to a finish.

Muffled groans of relief from the prospects. The opportunity meeting was over.

The prospects' final response?

To flee to their cars the instant the meeting finished.

Best intentions are meaningless without skills.

The clueless speaker had goals, a vision board, chanted affirmations, and sang the company song before starting the meeting. Shaking with enthusiasm, this over-motivated killer of prospects had the best intentions. He wanted to deliver the best opportunity meeting ever. He loved his business.

But getting our sales message from inside our heads to our prospects' heads takes skills. Our speaker didn't know this, and failed everyone in the room.

Yes, failure is an option.

But we don't want that option.

What should we do when failure is not an option?

We learn the skills to get our message across to others, with the purpose of getting a "yes" decision.

While some people may think this is an art, the good news is that it is a skill. Anyone can learn to do this. Let's start now.

IT IS ALL ABOUT THE BRAIN.

The big picture is simple.

1. Our prospects' brains receive our message (sometimes).

2. Then our prospects' brains make a decision (always).

First, the message.

Have you ever talked to someone, but felt like nobody was home? We saw our message crash against their forehead and fall to the floor, never once entering their brain. That is a bad feeling.

But let's not blame our prospects. It is not their fault. Their brains have programs to ignore almost everything. We must be better. We have to be impossible for our prospects to ignore.

There are millions of bits of data fighting for our prospects' attention. If we are not #1, their conscious minds will ignore us. Second place is not good enough.

Much of this book is about getting that attention, and implanting our message in our prospects' memories.

Second, the decision.

This is harder. Brains are complicated. So we will also take a look at how the mind works.

When we understand some basic mind rules, our ability to get "yes" decisions will improve. We won't go home and say to ourselves, "I don't know why they didn't want to join. This was perfect for them."

Mind rules? Yes. We didn't study this in school, and we did not learn this in our jobs. But ignorance is no excuse. The universe has a rule. It says, "If we are going to be stupid, we are going to get punished."

Now would be a great time for us to learn some basic brain rules. Not only will sponsoring and selling be easy, but we won't go home scratching our heads wondering what happened.

Getting "yes" decisions feels great. We can make this happen.

Let's begin by taking a look at the brain. The more we understand the brain, the easier it will be for us to adjust how we talk to people.

How do our brains make decisions?

Shouldn't this be the most important question in our profession?

As we mentioned earlier, our job is to get "yes" decisions from prospects. That is what our companies pay us to do.

There are no bonuses for being motivated, cutting out pictures for our vision board, sending people to websites, and getting prospects to make "no" decisions.

We have one job. Get prospects to join our business or be customers.

The good news is that our companies have to do everything else. This means we can concentrate on getting "yes" decisions.

But back to the original question, "How do our brains make decisions?"

If we didn't ask this question, and had no idea how our brains work, we would look silly. We would approach potential prospects and wouldn't know where or how to start our conversation.

Consider this conversation with a prospective distributor:

Us: "Please join my business."

Prospect: "What do you do?"

Us: "I get 'yes' decisions from prospects. I have no idea how it works. Do you want to join?"

Wow. Maybe that is why prospects don't join our business.

Or, how about this conversation at a party?

Stranger: "So what do you do for a living?"

Us: "I am in the decision-making business. I have no idea how it works."

Stranger: "Oh."

Can we build our network marketing business without learning anything about what we are doing? Yes. It has been done. But the road is long, frustrating, and very, very hard. We don't want to wait years for results.

Prospects are smart. They can sense incompetency and smell desperation. We don't need this painful handicap.

A better plan? Reduce our pain by learning a few guidelines about how our brains work.

DECISIONS, DECISIONS, DECISIONS.

Overlooking bad biology, here is a metaphor that helps us understand our minds.

This is a gross oversimplification, but we need to make sense of how our prospects make decisions.

The conscious mind.

Imagine a small green pea. This will represent our conscious mind.

This is the part of our mind that we use to learn new things, listen to lectures, and figure things out. The keyword is, "Think."

If we see something new or unfamiliar, we have to think. Is this new thing dangerous? Will it eat me? Or, can I eat it? What is going on?

This part of the brain is great for learning new things. You are using it now while reading this book.

The conscious mind uses a lot of energy. Remember this. It will be important later.

Imagine we are studying hard for an exam. Even though we're just sitting, don't we feel tired after a few hours? Using the conscious mind burns up a lot of precious energy.

Sitting and thinking is sort of like working out, but without the sweat. When we think hard for a long time, we say, "I am mentally exhausted! Now all I want to do is zone out and watch television."

Children know this. When they want to ask a favor from Mom and Dad, they wait until later in the day. They know their parents feel tired from thinking all day, and are vulnerable to their skilled requests for sugar.

This part of the mind is optimized for thinking. It is not good at making decisions. Why?

#1. It is too slow.

If we use this part of our minds to make our decisions, we would die. Think about it. We make over 100,000 decisions every second just to stay alive. Blink this eye, create 30,000 new digestive enzymes, pump blood over here, move this muscle, create more T4 cells, time for our heart to beat, which ventricle do we open first, don't forget about breathing, and more.

And these are decisions just to stay alive! Thankfully, another part of our mind makes all of these decisions for us.

Imagine this scenario. We trip on a rock and start falling face-first to the pavement. We don't want our conscious mind to be trying to decide what to do.

It might say to itself, "The pavement appears to be approaching my face rapidly. My face is unprotected. Maybe I should do something about this. Maybe I should activate one of the muscles in my arms to start moving my hand to protect my face. Yes, that would be a good protective measure. Let's send a signal to the appropriate muscles to engage in this activity."

Splat!

Thinking is slow. Thinking enough to make a decision is way too slow. Nothing would get done.

#2. It is too small.

The conscious part of our minds can only have one thought at a time. That is it.

Can it multitask? Not really.

Our mind can switch back and forth, but that takes precious transition time. To prove this, we could try this dangerous experiment. Please do it someplace safe.

Try to multiply two large numbers mentally, while two people talk to us simultaneously about different things, while we drive our car on a high-speed obstacle course. This is not going to end well.

Our conscious mind has limits. One thought at a time. No multitasking.

This means our conscious minds have the constant stress of hundreds or thousands of decisions queuing up waiting for a turn. Want to see our reaction to this?

Someone calls us for an appointment to show their network marketing business. This person says, "I only need 30 minutes of your time."

Our conscious mind panics. "What? 30 minutes! I can't even give you 30 seconds. I have so many decisions to make." This explains why getting appointments is difficult.

#3. Limited memory.

If someone reads a list of random words, we can remember the most recent words. Next, this person reads another list of random words. We start to forget the original list of words as more words are added. The words are falling out of the back of our memory as fast as we are putting them in.

There are memory tricks to help, but we don't want to waste our day on memory tricks for useless, random words.

How does this shortage of memory apply to our business?

Remember those presentations with information overload? The presentations where we talked way too much? The presentations that made our prospects' eyes glaze over?

New information to our conscious mind must be paced. It takes time for our conscious minds to digest this new information and understand it. Even then, only a little bit of this new information will go to the memory.

Most of the time, we present too much information too quickly in network marketing. Our prospects' conscious minds can't keep up. As we dump more and more information and benefits, our prospects forget the good things we said earlier.

#4. No authority.

Even if our conscious mind thinks that it made a decision, it gets overruled by our subconscious mind. Let's take a look at a slow, thought-out decision by our conscious mind.

"It is New Year's Eve. Time to make my New Year's resolutions. Starting tomorrow I will go to the gym and work out every day, while eating healthy fruits and vegetables. I will lose 15 pounds by the end of the month. I am tired of this flabby waistline. When the people at work make fun of me, I feel bad. This is my time to shine. I can do this!"

Yes, our conscious mind has made a great decision.

Then, on New Year's morning our subconscious mind steps in and says one word:

"Donuts!"

Our powerful subconscious mind takes the pea-sized conscious mind and puts it into the palm of its hand. Then it takes a thumb and finger and flicks the pea off the hand, never to be seen again.

The subconscious mind is fortified with armored programs that crush decisions by the conscious mind. The reality? Our conscious mind only has hopes, wishes, and suggestions.

We might think, "It appears that the conscious mind is there for entertainment purposes only."

Harsh. But when we talk about decisions, this might not be too far from the truth.

Okay, the conscious mind is for thinking and new information. Now we can now go to the other part of the brain, the subconscious mind.

THE SUBCONSCIOUS MIND.

If the conscious mind is the size of a pea, then by comparison, the subconscious mind would be the size of this world. An exaggeration, but we get the idea.

Before we feel intimidated, here is an easy way to look at the subconscious mind. Consider the subconscious mind as a collection of:

- Shortcuts for stuff we do every day.
- Automatic programs. For example, if this happens, then automatically do this.
- Stored emotions and drama from our childhood.
- Prejudices.
- Memories.
- All of the decisions we make, so when a familiar situation comes up, we already have a decision for it. We won't have to rethink it.

Here are some simplified subconscious mind basics.

#1. This part of the mind does not think.

"Thinking" is for the conscious mind. For the subconscious mind, imagine a machine that simply processes automatic programs.

There will be no thinking in this part of the brain. Why? Because it already has the conscious part of the mind to do the thinking and learning. Instead, the subconscious mind does **everything else** for us in life.

Everything else? Pretty much.

How is that possible?

Thinking takes a lot of work and time. The conscious part of our mind handles that. So, the subconscious mind doesn't have to work hard at thinking.

But automatic programs? Easy. They just happen. No thinking involved.

This is why the subconscious mind can multitask with hundreds of thousands of programs automatically. This part of our mind is a true multitasker.

#2. The subconscious mind has millions of programs.

Millions? Well, a lot. No one knows for sure.

Where did we get these automatic programs? From:

- Parents. They told us what to think and do.
- Teachers. They told us what to think and do.
- The news. They choose which stories we see, and which viewpoints are presented.
- Friends. They tell us what to think to "fit in" with the group.
- Bad personal experiences. Ever get stung by a bee? Now we have a program about bees.
- Good experiences.

- Books we read.

- Television programs we watch.

- We are born with some programs installed: programs such as a fear of loud noises, fear of falling, curiosity, and survival. We rapidly add to these programs as we try to learn how to survive in our world.

There are more, but we get the idea.

Most of our programs were dumped into our minds by others.

The subconscious mind is the giant warehouse that stores and executes these programs.

#3. If something happens, then these programs say, "Do this."

There is no judgment or reflection involved. Our subconscious mind just executes the current resident program.

- If we fall forward, throw up our hands to protect our faces.

- If we took a breath five seconds ago, how about another breath now?

- If a large puddle of water is in our path, walk around it.

- Left foot, then the right foot.

- If we are sitting, constantly adjust the muscles in our sides so we don't fall over.

- If we stub our toe, yell!

- If we finish chewing, swallow.

- If someone shouts our name, turn and look in that direction.

- If we lose our wallet or purse, feel upset and sad.

- If we forget our password, get frustrated.

- If we meet someone who doesn't smile, be cautious.

- If our stomach growls, eat more snacks.

- If that driver swerves in front of me, avoid the collision and honk the horn.

- If it itches, scratch.

- If I have a wound, send some antibodies over to kill any infection.

Unfortunately, most of our prospects will have these resident programs in their subconscious minds:

- If they look like salespeople, don't believe anything.

- If someone asks too many questions, be careful.

- If a salesman asks us to agree, hold back. The salesman will use our agreement against us.

- If someone asks for an appointment, that person will try to sell me something I don't want.

- Delay all decisions. We don't want to make the wrong choice.

#4. These programs don't cover everything.

Our conscious mind can only focus on one thing at a time. Our subconscious mind has to do everything else.

Then, what happens when the subconscious mind doesn't have a program for something?

It does the best it can.

Here is an example. We come home from work, and our conscious mind is thinking about what to watch on television tonight. As we reach into the refrigerator for food, our car keys are still in our right hand. What will the subconscious mind do? It doesn't have a program for "reaching for food with car keys in the right hand."

It does the best it can. It says, "Car keys go on a flat surface. This will do." That is why we can't find our car keys the next morning. Our car keys are in the refrigerator.

Or, think about our dreams. Our subconscious mind controls our dreaming, and what a mess that is. Thankfully, we don't have to live our dreams.

Our subconscious mind isn't perfect for handling all our day-to-day tasks, but it does a pretty good job. Since we are reading this book, we are still alive. Our subconscious mind is doing okay so far.

#5. Autopilot.

Yes, we can go through life on autopilot. Every day we go through the motions of living, reacting to what happens to us. Our subconscious minds have programs to tell us what to do next in these situations.

Autopilot? Unfortunately, yes.

Most people will do the same things today that did not work for them yesterday. For example, maybe they hate their job. What do they do today? Instead of looking for a new job that could give them more happiness, they go back to the job they hate. This routine continues.

People rarely stop to evaluate their habits and patterns. It is easier to continue doing the same thing over and over. That is why it is difficult for us to get prospects to make a change. They are stuck in their cycle, and will continue in that cycle unless we have the skills to help them change.

Past behavior is the most reliable predictor of future behavior. Sad, but true.

Want an example of this pattern of automatic decisions running our lives? Let's take a drive.

We drive our usual 45-minute commute to work one morning. Our conscious mind listens to the depressing lyrics of country-western music. Occasionally our mind drifts to the television show we watched last night. Now if our conscious mind is busy with music and some memories, who is driving our car?

The answer? Our subconscious minds.

Through years of programming, we developed many automatic programs for driving.

"Don't cross the yellow line. Death is inconvenient."

"Stay in the lane. We could get nails in our tires from the shoulder of the road."

"Don't go too fast. We don't want a speeding ticket."

We are driving on autopilot. We could pull into the parking lot at work and not remember any details of our journey. Our subconscious mind handled everything.

Or how about this? We change jobs.

We find ourselves automatically driving the old route to work if we don't pay attention. Programs and habits are powerful.

Let's take a walk.

We are nine months old. We pull ourselves up in our crib, and then what? We lock our left leg into position. We have a death grip on our crib. But we want to walk.

Our conscious mind looks down and says, "Look! You've got a right leg. Let's swing that around and see what happens."

We try, fail, try, fail, and eventually get it right. All of these conscious repetitions form a program in our subconscious mind. Now when we walk, we don't have to think about it. You don't see people walking down the street mumbling, "Left foot, then the right foot." It is automatic.

Think of how many decisions our subconscious minds make just to walk.

Activate these muscles 60%. Bend the left knee 34 degrees. Activate the calf muscles. Bend ankle 45 degrees. Shift weight 62%. Activate the balancing muscle on the left hip. Release stimulus to the calf muscle on the left leg. Etc.

All of these actions are controlled by our pre-existing subconscious mind programs.

The subconscious mind is a decision-making machine!

In a way, our entire lives are on autopilot with brief moments of consciousness.

Now for some Exciting News!

We are in control of our prospecting experiences.

Let's look at the facts.

1. Our prospects' subconscious minds make their decisions.

2. Our prospects' subconscious minds do not think. They only react.

3. React to what? Us.

4. So if we want our prospects to react in a certain way, all we have to do is change what we say and do.

Awesome!

This means we are not unfortunate victims of the whims of our prospects. Our input makes a huge difference in the result.

The good news? By changing what we say and do, we can change our results.

The bad news? We don't know what to say and do when we first start our network marketing careers. But, we can learn. We can learn how our prospects' minds work and adjust our message.

Prospecting and closing can be within our control. Every time? No.

But most of the time our influence will be enough to deliver our message effectively.

We don't know what happened to our prospect one hour earlier. And we don't know if our products or opportunity are a good fit or not. But we will do what we do best - deliver our message with the best chance of success.

What's next?

We now have a basic understanding of our prospects' minds.

Subconscious mind programs control our prospects.

These programs make decisions for our prospects.

We want to talk to these programs.

The first part of our challenge is over, learning how our prospects think and make decisions.

The second part of our challenge is learning what we can say and do to get "yes" decisions.

Getting our message heard and remembered.

Here is where it all goes wrong.

We talk, no one listens.

We have the false belief that if we say something, other people care. The reality?

People don't care about us, and they care even less about our stuff. When we present our message, it is easy for our prospects to ignore it. They have plenty of experience ignoring almost everything.

Our subconscious minds have a filter that keeps unimportant, extraneous information from entering our brains. Yes, this filter will keep us out also. We have to work hard to get inside our prospects' minds.

If our prospects don't pay attention to us, there is no chance that our message will be heard.

How do we break out of this clutter of ignored information?

We accept that the brain skims information.

Our brains ignore 99.9% of what it takes in. There isn't enough room or enough time to encode every detail, fact, and nuance to memory.

Our brain's solution?

It has a gateway program that filters out unnecessary stuff. It filters out almost everything!

- Details.

- Colors.

- Stuff not moving.

- Non-essential elements.

- Sounds.

- And even us.

Us???

Ouch! If we are not interesting or noteworthy, we become just one more person in a crowd.

Imagine this. We walk down a crowded street in New York City. We walk past 3,000 people. What do we remember about those 3,000 people?

Nothing.

We attend a three-hour lecture. How much do we remember immediately after it is over? Maybe only two- or three-minutes' worth of new information! 98% of the lecture is already gone.

Psychologist Hermann Ebbinghaus documented this over 100 years ago. He called this the "forgetting curve." It was a curved graph that showed we forget:

- 50% in one hour.

- 70% after one day.

- 90% after one week.

This is an approximation, but today? We have the Internet, endless advertisements, messages, notifications, and more. With our information overload, Ebbinghaus would be an optimist with these numbers. Let's test it.

Give a one-hour presentation. Then, one hour later, ask the prospect to tell you everything he remembered. After one or two minutes of repeating what he remembered … silence.

Looks like 98% is either not heard or forgotten in one hour.

That means in a one-hour presentation, our prospects won't remember those 64 PowerPoint slides. If we are lucky, our prospects remember one or two slides. Sure, we wish this wasn't true, but this is reality.

So, our prospects remember a few slides or a few minutes of what we say. Shouldn't we make sure that we have a clear message in those slides or minutes?

Depressed? This is normal.

Our very normal brains will forget. Why should we remember what door we used to enter the shopping mall last Thursday? Why should we remember where we parked the car three months ago?

But what if we want our prospects to pay attention, listen, internalize, and remember what we say? We will need strategies that work with our prospects' minds.

Here is what our companies may not have told us.

We have to do more than show prospects a set of PowerPoint slides or a company video.

The company doesn't need us to do this. They could simply post everything on the Internet.

Instead, the company wants us to use our most important asset. What is that asset?

Our ability to get prospects to listen to us and believe us. This is something companies cannot do.

We don't want to be talking parrots. We must use our best skills to deliver our message. If we fail, our message is lost in the sea of chatter that prospects hear daily.

Brain science gives us effective strategies to bypass the negative programs, the salesman alarms, the too-good-to-be-true filters, and the negativity of our prospects.

Let's learn some strategies to get our message heard and internalized.

STRATEGY #1:
NO DUMPING ALLOWED!

Wishing that prospects would hear our message is useless. We become part of the blur of information passing by their brains every day.

Instead of dumping all of our information at once, we need to deliver small bites of information. Then, pause to let the conscious mind process the meaning. Too much information at one time ends up being overwhelming.

Not only do prospects' minds have to store what we say, they have to look for meaning. "Why is this information important to me? Should I pay attention to it? Would I want to remember it? Does the presenter have an agenda?"

Our minds want **meaning** first and then the **details** later. If we give details first, all of these questions get in the way. So we must go slowly. A ten-minute or one-hour monologue of information will be ugly. Our prospects will forget our information as fast as we deliver it.

What can we do to make our message heard?

Start with the meaning of the message. Why is our message important? The details can come later.

Humans make instant decisions. If the decision is "yes," then their brains welcome the details. But first give them a second or two to make their decisions. Here is an example.

Us: "Are you hungry?"

Prospect: "Yes."

Now we can give the details of the restaurant we recommend for lunch.

For our business, our ice breaker can give our prospects a chance to decide if they are interested or not. Then, if the answer is "yes," we deliver the details. An example:

Us: "Did you ever want to be your own boss?" (Ice breaker. Our prospect searched his subconscious mind for pre-made decisions about his boss. Found one. Took a microsecond.)

Prospect: "Yes! My idiot boss didn't give me a raise and I hate commuting for two hours every day." (Decision.)

Us: "Would it be okay if we have a cup of coffee with Joe and he can show you how he started working from home?" (Details.)

Notice how we are pacing the information? A short opening. The prospect has a chance to digest our information. And then we continue.

This is ultra-brief, but monologue information dumps don't work. Plan some breaks in our presentations. Take a deep breath. Show a demonstration or sample to break up an intense data dump.

The result? If our prospects have a bit more time to digest what we say, they will remember more.

We need to be polite to our prospects. Give them the meaning of our message before we give them the details of our message. This will put their minds at ease and they can listen to our message comfortably.

STRATEGY #2:
QUESTIONS.

Questions force our prospect to think of an answer.

This means our message stays longer in their brains and gets attention too. Consider this short conversation:

Us: "We need Vitamin D. But of the two different types of Vitamin D, which one is more effective?"

Prospect: "I've never thought about it. I didn't even know there were two types of Vitamin D. Which one is the best?"

Our prospect now thinks this is important and that he should remember it.

This is better than a fact dump saying, "Our Vitamin D3 is better for you than Vitamin D2."

Another scenario:

We could say, "Our multivitamin has lots of Vitamin K."

This ends up as extra noise. We will be ignored. But what if we said this instead?

"We need Vitamin K to be healthy. But let me show you a picture of two avocados. Can you tell which one contains more Vitamin K?"

Of course our prospects can't. This creates doubt. If our prospects want to be healthy, our multivitamin with Vitamin K appears to be the only solution. The decision and sale will be easy.

And even if we don't make the sale right away, our prospects will think about Vitamin K every time they see an avocado. Our message spends more time in their minds.

We take advantage of repeated exposure and time-released repetition to implant our message into our prospects' brains.

Our prospects think about what this means to them. They internally answer these questions. This extra engagement helps our message to enter their awareness and possibly even their memory.

How about some more examples?

Us: "Do you know how much they are currently overcharging you on your electricity bill?"

Prospect: "No. I never look at it. But sounds like I am being overcharged, huh?"

We slowed down our prospect's thinking. Before, our prospect didn't want to think about it. Now he wants to know. As we investigate the overcharges, we extend his interest. More time equals a better chance that our prospect will remember this.

Ready for more great questions to get our prospects to internalize our message?

Us: "Here are two cups of tea. One is green tea. One is matcha tea. Can you tell which cup has 300% more antioxidants? Which cup has twice the caffeine?"

Prospect: "Uh, no. I don't know."

Now our prospect is thinking about our benefits. Instead of mentioning our wonderful benefits, our prospect is asking himself which tea is better for him.

More?

Us: "You might find this interesting. If our current job ends, and no more paychecks come in, how many days will pass before we are in trouble?"

Prospect: "I don't know. I never thought about it."

Us: "Give it your best guess. Let's see if it is more or less than the national average."

Now our prospect has to think even more.

Us: "They say we need $1.5 million when we retire. If you start now, at your age, how much money would you have to put into your savings account every month to get there?"

Prospect: "I don't know."

Us: "Take your best guess and see if you can guess within $200."

The longer we can keep the prospect engaged with this thought, the better.

If we can, avoid questions that have a one-word answer. We want to stretch out our time inside our prospect's brain. So instead of asking for one option in the answer, we can ask for two options. Here is an example.

Us: "If you didn't have to commute an hour coming home from work every day, list two things you would do."

Prospect: "Let me think. I could attend my son's games and some days have time for 9 holes of golf before the sun went down."

***

Us: "If you had a chance to work out of your home instead of commuting to a job, what are the first two things you would do with your family?"

Prospect: "Well, we could spend more weekends camping. We could leave right after school on Friday afternoon. And second? We could have breakfast and dinner together as a family."

***

Us: "If your electricity bill next month was $30 lower, would you still send the extra $30 to your electricity company because you felt guilty? What would you do with the extra $30? Any ideas?"

Prospect: "Of course I wouldn't send them extra money. I would spend it on my daughter. I would add $30 to her allowance. She would love me for that."

Let our prospects sell themselves.

How? With questions, of course. Ask them why they would consider what we are about to offer.

For our prospects to answer, they have to convince themselves of the benefits. To understand this better, let's give some examples.

Us: "Why would you want an extra income for your family?"

Prospect: "By the time we pay the mortgage, both car payments, school fees, and our other monthly expenses, we end up in the negative. This puts us further into debt. We know an extra few hundred dollars every month will fix this."

By answering this question, our prospects "sell themselves" as we listen. Now when we present our solution, it will be easy.

How about this?

Us: "Why do you want better holidays?"

Prospect: "For our last holiday, we booked the cheapest accommodations we could find. It was a nightmare. Ruined our holiday. We want to save money, but it is hard to find good value when we are on a tight budget."

Presenting our high-value travel package at a discount is easy now.

The question is simple. Ask our prospects why they would want to buy what we offer. Ask them to convince themselves before we start.

"What are your two biggest _____ problems?"

Why is this question so powerful? Let's consider an easy nutritional products example.

Older people buy nutritional products. Young people feel just fine.

Go to a party that includes older people. In a conversation, ask this question:

"What are your two biggest health problems?"

The prospects smile. They have an audience. Everyone else they know hates listening to them complain about their aches and pains.

They love us. They think we are the greatest person in the world because we listen.

And when the prospects finally take a breath from their health complaints, ask them, "Do you want to do something about it?" Or, "Have you ever considered doing something about it?"

It's easy to sell nutritional products to someone complaining about their health.

This is a "license to print money" technique.

Some quick examples of this question:

"What are your two biggest problems when you travel?"

"What are your two biggest problems when you have to commute every day to work?"

"What are your two biggest problems with trying to stay on a diet?"

"What are your two biggest problems when trying to figure out the right skincare products to use?"

"What are your two biggest problems with trying to save for retirement?"

Then stand back. Listen. And let our prospects tell us exactly what they want us to fix.

STRATEGY #3:
WHAT IS BETTER
THAN QUESTIONS?

We talk to our prospects about things that interest them. Yes, it is all about them, not about us.

How do we get prospects to talk to us? Questions work great. But as we will see, indirect statements work even better.

Think about the negative programs in our prospects' minds. When we were children, what happened when we did something wrong? Our parents interrogated us. Our parents would ask, "Why did you do this? What were you thinking?"

Our reaction to this interrogation? Fear. We didn't reveal our true feelings and motivation to our parents. We created a program, "Avoid interrogation."

We often ask questions to understand our prospects' motivation. Unfortunately, our prospects don't hear these questions as motivation-finding questions. Instead, our prospects activate their old fear programs. They think, "Don't say what I'm actually thinking. Be careful. Don't expose myself. This may be the wrong answer. Be careful, because a salesman might use this against me."

We want to help. Our prospects fear our questions.

So instead of asking questions, let's try this.

Indirect statements.

Here is an example of a direct question. "How much money do you want to earn with our business?"

Our prospect feels interrogated and withdraws emotionally.

A better approach is to use an indirect statement.

We could say, "I don't know how much money you would want to make with our business."

This statement feels safe to our prospects. Their subconscious minds interpret our statement as, "How much money do you want to make with our business?"

Now they may volunteer that information with no further prompting from us. In many cases, our prospects will volunteer even more information than we asked for.

Indirect statements feel safe and polite. Let's try another example.

Us: "I don't know how much weight you would like to lose with our product."

Our prospect hears and interprets this as, "How much weight do you want to lose with our product?"

Here is an extra benefit. When our prospects answer, they can only make sense of our statement by visualizing themselves using our product. This helps our prospects make a decision to use our product. They already saw themselves using our product in their brains. Our product becomes more familiar.

This sounds like fun. No chance of objections or rejection.

Let's do some examples to kickstart our imaginations.

"I don't know how much younger you want your skin to look by using our special moisturizer."

"I don't know how much you want to help the environment by using non-chemical cleaners."

"I don't know how much you want to save on your cell-phone bill, but I am sure you could think of fun things to do with the savings."

"I don't know how much you want to save on your electricity bill, but I am sure you want to get rid of the overpayments now."

"I don't know how much you value memories from your family holidays, but this will certainly improve the experience."

"I don't know how happy you would be if you had more money to spend on what you want."

"I don't know how important it is to your children to experience a week at Disney World."

"I don't know how much better off your family would be if you had more time to spend with them."

"I don't know how important your personal health is to you."

"I don't know what you would do if you could get rid of your alarm clock."

"I don't know what losing 30 pounds will mean to you."

"I don't know how you will feel going to the class reunion looking young and vibrant, unlike those older classmates."

"I don't know what you would do with time freedom, never having to show up to work again."

"I don't know when it will be a good time for you to start having a second paycheck."

"I don't know how much you hate leaving your family for the job, but I do know you want more quality time with your children."

"I don't know if they are overpaying you at work or not, but I do know our business can add a lot of extra money each month."

"I don't know if you want to be your own boss or not, but I do know most people would like more control over the hours they work."

"I don't know how you feel about cars and monthly car payments, but our car bonus qualifiers enjoy never having to make another car payment again."

No pressure. Our prospects volunteer answers, even though we didn't ask a question.

Will this work for most products and services? Yes!

A networker who sells his services to help homeowners get fairer insurance claims asked, "Will this work for my business?" Of course. Here are some examples we created.

"I don't know how you feel about facing your homeowner's insurance company by yourself, instead of letting me help you ..."

"I don't know how confident you are in making a claim to your homeowner's insurance without me to help you ..."

"I don't know how you would feel about me helping you with your insurance claim ..."

"I don't know what outcome you would expect with me helping you prepare and present your insurance claim ..."

What other starter words could we use to deliver our messages in an indirect way?

"I think you already know."

When we say, "I think you already know," even if our prospects don't know, they will know now. They hear our message. This is a good way to transfer some of our best sales messages into skeptical prospects' minds. Here are some examples.

"I think you already know that we have the lowest rates."

"I think you already know that last year we were voted the #1 vacation travel value."

"I think you already know that your identity has already been stolen, and the criminals are waiting for the best time to sell it."

"I think you already know that our bodies need antioxidants to slow down the aging process."

"I think you already know the best way to fight wrinkles is from the inside."

"I think you already know that companies place profit first. They have to be responsible to the shareholders."

"I think you already know that our commuting time is lost forever. We will never get that time back."

"I think you already know that smart people don't put all their income in one basket."

"I think you already know how much time our jobs take from our week."

"I think you already know that if we try hard and work overtime, only our boss gets a big house for his retirement."

"I think you already know that our pensions won't be enough to let us do what we want."

"I think you already know that we don't want to work corporate jobs for 45 years like our parents."

"I think you already know that research shows that diets don't work."

"I think you already know that prices go up faster than our paychecks."

"I think you already know that nothing will change in our lives unless we change what we do."

"I think you already know that closed-minded people never get the success they want."

"I think you already know that living paycheck-to-paycheck feels like a dead end."

"I think you already know that having more money gives us more options."

Even the most skeptical prospects still hear these indirect statements. It's a great way to deliver our message without stressing our prospects.

And what about our friend who sells his services to help homeowners get better insurance settlements?

"I think you already know that people who use us to present their homeowner's claim have better payouts."

"I think you already know that people who let us help them in a homeowner's claim have less stress."

"I think you already know that people hate dealing with insurance companies and would rather let us help them."

STRATEGY #4:
THE SCIENCE OF SHORT.

Here is another way to look at our brains.

Imagine our brain as a giant battery.

If our battery runs down, we can't function. That means we become lion food on the savannah. So our brain watches our battery reserves as part of our survival program.

How much energy do our brains use? Some scientists estimate that our brains use 20% of our energy! That is a lot. So if we just sit around and think, the good news is that we are sort of exercising and working out.

Think about the time in school when we studied hard for three hours. How did we feel after three hours of our conscious mind thinking, figuring things out, and trying to memorize things? We felt exhausted. Our conscious minds use a lot of energy.

Our subconscious minds use less energy. All the stored decisions in our subconscious minds are pre-made. We don't have to think about them anymore. Our subconscious minds have an easier job. They activate programs when needed. No hard thinking involved.

That means given a choice, we would prefer to use our subconscious minds' pre-made automatic programs and decisions. This is easier and more energy-efficient than figuring everything out again each time with our conscious minds. It is convenient and saves us time.

Let's go to the local grocery store. We have our cart and are about to go down aisle 4. As we walk down the aisle, we see hundreds of different products. Thankfully our subconscious mind has stored decisions about these products. We quickly go down the aisle saying, "No. No. No. Yes, I will take that box of donuts. No. No. That bottle of wine looks good. Yeah, I should take two bottles of wine. No. No. No." End of aisle 4.

If our subconscious minds did not have these stored decisions, and we had to think about every item, we would starve before we got to the end of aisle 4.

Here is another example. Someone offers us ice cream. Our conscious mind could work hard and think, "Let me calculate how much saturated fat is in that ice cream. I should look up the glycemic index. If I don't eat too much, the glycemic load will be less. Will that sugar affect my A1c? Would it be rude for me to refuse the ice cream?"

This is a lot of work for our conscious mind, and could burn a lot of energy. Thank goodness we have a pre-made decision on ice cream.

"Ice cream? I will take it!"

As we can see, our survival program tries to save energy by using the decisions stored in our subconscious minds. Survival first is the rule. If we don't survive, well, not much else matters.

Starting to feel the inevitable? The brain wants to make the quick and easy pre-made decisions whenever possible.

So how does that affect us?

Sometimes the brain makes a decision based upon conserving energy, and not what is good and bad. This explains some of our bad decisions. We made the easiest and quickest decision that our brains came up with.

This means our brains must make a quick choice:

#1. "Do I make the decision based upon whether this action is good or bad? This will take a lot of conscious mind battery life."

#2. "Instead, can I choose a pre-made program from the subconscious mind? That is an instant decision and we will save precious battery life."

Unfortunately, the answer is obvious. Our brain will take a subconscious mind's pre-made decision any chance it gets.

This is why willpower is so hard. Conscious mind decisions use a lot of energy and time, and we don't want to drain our battery. An example?

The giant beam of light.

A giant beam of light suddenly blinds us. Oh my! What could this be? Our subconscious mind flashes through the possibilities. We are not on railroad tracks, so it can't be a locomotive about to kill us. We didn't hear an explosion. Flashlights don't shine that brightly.

Our subconscious minds say, "I don't have anything."

Now it is up to our conscious minds to figure this out. We don't have any automatic programs that were easy explanations. Our conscious minds begin burning energy as it thinks, "Well, I am still alive. Wow, this is bright. I don't even see a shadow. I can't run. I can't see where I am going. But, if I stay here, it will be dangerous. I better reach out and feel my way out of here."

Our conscious mind works overtime. It burns energy. If we survive this, we will be exhausted from all this thinking. Thinking is hard work.

Here is where it could go very wrong for us.

We are 15 minutes into our one-hour presentation. Our prospect thinks,

"Should I start my own business? Wow. There is so much to consider here. What will my neighbors think? Will I be successful? How big is the market for these products and services? Do I have the skills? I am not sure I will understand the compensation plan. I see a chart with lots of numbers. Will this affect my relationship with my family? What if this doesn't work out and I fail? Oh my! So many things to think about, so many options. Let me check with my subconscious mind to see if I have a pre-made decision on starting my own business. That would save me a lot of energy and thinking. Hey look! I have a program that is somewhat close. I started my own business with a lemonade stand when I was six years old. It failed. I was humiliated. I don't like the risk of failure. I don't want to be in business. I will use that pre-made decision, so I won't have to do all this thinking. Let me turn off my mind and check my phone messages while they finish this meeting."

In this example, did our minds make a decision based on what is good for us or bad for us? Or did our minds make a decision based on conserving energy?

Yes. Sometimes our minds don't care if something is good or bad. It just wants to conserve energy.

This is the danger of talking too long. We want to keep our messages short so our prospects don't turn off their thinking and make snap decisions.

Here is another example.

A salesman comes to our home and begins a long, boring presentation. So many facts. So much proof. Videos, PowerPoint slides, and information overload. Our brains say, "This is going to take a lot of processing power. Do we have an easier decision we can make? Oh look! Here is an easy decision we don't have to think about. We don't like salesmen. Let's use that decision so we don't have to think about all this stuff. Listening more and thinking will use up too much energy."

The salesman thinks the decision is all about him and his offer.

Wrong!

The decision was to save battery life.

Ouch!

We think, "But that decision wasn't even related to the salesman's offer!"

True. But saving precious brain battery life has a higher priority than an extremely talkative salesman.

Unless we understand how the brain works, we won't have any idea what happened. We will be under the delusion that the decision was about us or our offer.

And this is why many distributors go home and say to their spouses, "I don't know why they didn't join."

We experience the energy-saving automatic programs when we exercise. Many joggers and runners talk about "getting into the zone." They don't have to think about anything. It is all automatic. This saves energy that they can use to jog and run longer.

This is one reason we have habits.

Habits are automatic decisions. Our habits are easy to do. No thinking involved. We go down the same neural pathways over and over again. Our habits become our natural behaviors.

Changing habits? Oh my, that will take a lot of conscious brain energy. Change is difficult. We don't need examples of how hard it is to change our habits. We experience this every day.

Bottom line? We want to make it **harder** for our prospects to keep their problems than to take our solutions. Prospects prefer the path of least resistance.

A few examples of how we can make it harder for our prospects to keep their problems? We can use the simple nine-word phrase, "So what is going to be easier for you?"

Us: "So what is going to be easier for you? To continue going to work every day, fighting the traffic you hate, and working at a job you have no patience for? Or, to start your own part-time business this evening, so next year you can work out of your home and be your own boss?"

Us: "So what is going to be easier for you? To continue exercising, eating funny foods, starving yourself, and watching the weight come back? Or, to lose weight one time with us, and keep that weight off forever?"

Us: "So what is going to be easier for you? To fix your finances by hoping you will get a 50% pay raise this year? Or to start this business now, so you can earn the extra money you need?"

Us: "So what is going to be easier for you? To continue overpaying your electricity bill every month? Or, to spend five minutes with me on the Internet to fix your rates?"

This is why short beats long when communicating with our prospects.

Leave out the details.

Our prospects don't want to listen to details. If they listened to all the details on the Internet, it would use up their entire lives. How do they choose which details to listen to?

By making a decision first.

Humans prefer to make decisions first. If the decision is "yes" to our message, then, and only then, do their minds welcome the details. Giving details first stresses the minds of our prospects.

Think about how we choose which articles to read in the newspaper. We make a decision, based upon the headline, if we want to read the article or not. Once we make the decision to read the article, we dive in and enjoy the details.

Good news for us! We don't have to worry about the details now. All we have to do is get a "yes" or "no" decision quickly.

Big companies with huge marketing departments know that short works. These companies work hard to make their marketing messages short. See if our minds remember any of these marketing messages.

Nike: "Just do it."

U.S. Army: "Be all that you can be."

Coca-Cola: "Things go better with Coke."

M&Ms Candy: "Melts in your mouth, not in your hands."

BMW: "The ultimate driving machine."

Wendy's: "Where's the beef?" (Old people will remember this.)

Winston: "Winston tastes good like a cigarette should." (Only really old people will remember this.)

Kentucky Fried Chicken: "Finger-lickin' good."

Energizer Batteries: "Keeps going and going and going."

Not much on details, right?

We don't have the advantage of big corporate marketing budgets. And, we don't have years of repetition of our message to fall back on. Our message is brand-new to our prospects. That means we will need more than just a few words.

Let's take a look at what we can do with three or four short messages. These messages might take just a few seconds to say. Then, our prospects can make a quick "yes" or "no" decision.

The $21 Diet Test.

Never diet again.

Willpower in a pill.

Our prospects can make a decision now, and get more details next. If they wanted to lose weight based upon this message, they would welcome more details. The decision happened that fast.

Can we make our marketing and sales messages short and clear like this? Yes. Our prospects will love it when we get to the point immediately.

Where could we use this marketing message?

- When we have a booth at a tradeshow or exhibition. We only get seconds to talk to visitors.

- When we try to get an appointment and the person asks, "What is it all about?" They want real answers, not some vague generalities.

- If someone asks us at a networking event, "What do you sell?" If we get our message right, prospects will remember our it.

- On the back of our business card. That is free advertising space for us.

- To explain to anyone what we do. Prospects are happy that we finish in just a few seconds.

- To prequalify prospects before we invest time on the details. If they say, "Tell me more," it doesn't get any easier than that.

Creating a short marketing message is one of the best investments in our business. Let's take time now to look at some sample marketing messages to help our creativity.

For legal services:

Your personal lawyer guardian angel.

$35 a month, 24 hours a day.

Never be cheated again.

Custom vitamins:

Custom vitamins for your body.

Never waste money on vitamins again.

Feel the difference in seven days.

Travel:

Travel like a millionaire.

Pay like a cheapskate.

Make your Facebook friends jealous.

Utilities:

Save on your electricity bill.

Let your neighbors save big also.

Get paid when they turn on their lights.

Skincare:

Iron your wrinkles away.

Make your face your best first impression.

Never be called the "older sister" again.

Work from home:

No more alarms.

Wake up when you are ready.

Spend time working, not commuting.

Natural cleaners:

Safe cleaners for your home.

No fumes or lung damage.

Save our precious environment.

Boss-haters:

Be your own boss.

Set your own hours.

Only take orders from yourself.

Youth-seekers:

Growing old hurts.

Stop aging now.

Feel 16 years old again, but with better judgment.

Energy:

Stop feeling tired.

Only 15 minutes away from feeling great.

Healthy energy without caffeine.

For a business opportunity:

Hate commuting to work?

Start our part-time business at your home.

No risk.

Next year, work out of your home full-time.

Let's ask ourselves, "Which do we like best? A long presentation or a short presentation?"

Our answer? "We like a short presentation." That gives us a chance to say "yes" or "no" early in the conversation, and save our precious time. And if the short presentation interests us? We will happily ask for more details and a longer presentation.

Prospects feel the same way.

Prospects love to buy, but they hate to be sold. Shouldn't we make it easy for them to buy by making our presentation short instead of long?

If we can't explain how our products or services can solve a problem for our prospects in three sentences, this could be our problem!

Prospects don't want to wait around while we try to be clear and explain the details. They want the punchline now.

The "Hick's Law" trap.

Keep it simple. Why?

Hick's Law states that the more choices we give our prospects, the harder it becomes for them to make decisions.

Our brains are lazy. Too many choices mean our prospects have to think too hard to make up their minds.

Short and simple works. Prospects love it.

There is an old motivational saying in network marketing:

"If we are on fire, some people will come just to see us burn."

Might be true. So let's make sure we have something short and good to say while burning.

Use this shortcut.

Imagine that the brain has a program that says, "If it is simple, then it is right."

Our brains crave simplicity. They will want to believe that the simplest explanation and solution is correct.

More proof and more information is counterproductive.

Let's keep things short.

Strategy #5:
Emotion is our
prospect's friend.

This is the big one.

Grab your highlighter. Let's get started.

Psychologist Paul Ekman lists six basic emotions:

- Happiness (Yeah! Everyone wants this.)

- Sadness (The opposite.)

- Fear (Think snakes or nightmares.)

- Disgust (Long opportunity meetings and vegan cheese.)

- Anger (Our prospect didn't show up.)

- Surprise (We win the Oscar for Best Sponsor.)

We have programs about these emotions in our subconscious minds. These programs cause us to want things, or to avoid things.

Think of emotions as the triggers that make us do things.

No emotion. What happens? Nothing. We sit and do nothing until we experience an emotion.

Our emotions put us into action. We need emotions.

And decisions need emotions. More about that in a moment. But first, let's list more emotions:

- Trust (This is huge for our business when we talk to prospects.)
- Anticipation (Waiting for our birthday gifts or the new product announcement.)
- Shame (Everyone hates embarrassment.)
- Despair (When someone gives up hope and stops trying.)
- Love (Possibly the most sought-after emotion.)
- Horror (When we thought we qualified for the trip, but didn't.)
- Craving (Takes up 99% of starving dieters' brain activity.)
- Boredom (Usually induced by long, unwanted sales presentations.)
- Anxiety (The month is longer than the paycheck.)

Are there more emotions? Yes. The list could go on and on. But most of the emotions can be described as combinations of the basic emotions above.

Where do these emotions come from?

Our brain interprets what's going on around us. It uses what we sense, some past memories, and our current programs and creates an emotion. For example, we see a child crying. We remember the time when we cried as a child. Why did we cry? Because our mother scolded us. And now we are feeling very sad about this crying child.

If our prospect is feeling sad, he may make the decision to put off starting our business. On the other hand, if our prospect is angry at his boss, his decision may be immediate to get started now.

Emotion is necessary for decisions.

But the real question is this:

"Do humans use emotion or logic to make decisions?"

While information has value, it is not enough to close our prospects. We realize this when we dump information on prospects. So how does emotion fit into the decision-making process?

Here is the short version for our network marketing purposes:

Humans make decisions emotionally. Then ... they **dream up** some logical reasons to rationalize and justify those decisions.

We need emotions to make decisions.

Giving prospects facts, figures, slides, and videos will put their brains into analytical mode. Ouch. Now our prospects are disconnecting from the emotional, decision-making part of their brains. We need to rethink the videos and the PowerPoint presentations of our past.

Do we see the problem?

We create this problem by pushing our prospects into analytical mode. Yes, we are at fault.

Bottom line? Decisions are made emotionally ... and then justified or rationalized with logic. And that is how the brain works.

Here are some examples.

Why do you think someone buys our diet products?

Is it because of our patented amino-blend technology, the number of protein grams per serving, the fact that our doctor won an award somewhere, our company's shiny building, or our company founder's ability to walk on water when it is frozen?

Or do they buy our diet products to look good at the ten-year class reunion and to finally get a date?

Why do you think someone joins our business?

Because our company is ten years old and not nine years old? Because we had a 35% increase in sponsoring last month? Because our compensation plan pays 3% more on the PV of the BV of the GV?

Or, so they can earn enough money to stay home with their children instead of pawning them off to daycare?

So what is the goal of talking with our prospects?

A. To educate them with facts and figures.

B. To get a decision.

Our goal is to get "yes" decisions from our prospects. Let's stop showing PowerPoint slides, reciting research, and playing boring commercial videos. Instead, we will talk to the decision-making part of our prospects' brains with the emotional reasons to buy our products or to join our business.

Humans make emotional decisions. That is how it works. Later, we create a story to make us appear logical.

For example, that expensive red sports car.

Did the owner have this internal conversation? "They didn't make many of this model. I think it will hold its resale value over time. This makes a good investment, even though the gas mileage is terrible."

What is the more likely internal conversation? "I want it! It will make me look so cool! I've always wanted a fast, loud, red sports car that makes me look awesome."

Yes, that expensive red sports car is an emotional decision.

Do nerdy engineers make logical decisions?

Engineers make emotional decisions. Contrary to popular belief, engineers are human. Let's take this example.

The engineer receives quotes from contractors for the big city bridge. The engineer thinks:

"If I approve the lowest bid, and it doesn't work out, I will lose my job. I will lose my reputation. Then I can't support my family. It will be embarrassing for me to go out in public. I'd better take the higher bid from the established contractor so my life will not be ruined."

Decisions are … emotional.

Facts, figures, flipcharts, videos, and research should come after the decision. Why? Because after we make our emotional decision, we want to create a credible story that makes us appear logical.

The downside to emotional decisions.

Common sense? Logic? Yes, humans have these things. We see our friends make boneheaded decisions. We wish they would use common sense and logic. But no matter how long we analyze the data and manipulate the facts, it seems that emotions, not logic, will always trigger the decisions.

So if our job as networkers is to get decisions, what should our strategy be?

Up the emotion!

To increase the speed of a decision, all we need to do is to "up the emotion" in our prospects. Want an example?

Get angry.

Think of all the quick decisions we make when we are angry. Are these decisions thought out with green personality analytical logic? No. Let's take a look at a few angry decisions.

- "You hit me. I will hit you."
- "You took the money. I will shout at you."
- "You drive too slowly. I will honk my car's horn in anger."
- "My candidate did not win the election. I will drink beer all night."
- "My co-worker made fun of my weight. I will join the gym."
- "They asked if I was my sister's mother. I will buy this expensive skincare."
- "My relatives make fun of my car. I will work twice as hard in my business to earn the bonus car."

- "It took two hours of fighting traffic to get home. I will start my own home business."
- "The sink and the toilets don't work. I will never take a cheap holiday again."
- "This year-end bonus won't even pay for a nice evening out. I am going to look for another job."
- "My idiot brother-in-law only works four days a week now. I need to catch up."
- "My electricity bill is double what I paid last year. I need to switch now."
- "I spent four hours in the waiting room. I saw the doctor for three minutes. He recommended I go to another doctor's waiting room next week. I need to get well and take care of myself."
- "My grandchildren laughed when I couldn't remember. What can I do for my mind to help it remember?"
- "My mom told me to be home by 10PM. I am 31 years old. I need to pay off my student loans so I can get my own apartment."

None of these decisions took more than a few seconds. When emotions are high, decisions are easy. It is the lack of emotion that drags the decision-making process on and on. Did we notice the lack of facts, brochures, and presentations in these examples?

Anger is not the only emotion. We can have high levels of the other emotions we listed earlier. Think of the times we felt horror, craving, anticipation, love, or shame. Our emotions drove us to quick decisions at these times.

There is another benefit to emotions. Emotions create deeper memories in our prospects. When we think of past events, not only do our minds re-create the scenery or sequence of events, our minds also re-create the emotions we felt at that time.

What does this mean for us? When we "up the emotion" with our prospects, they will remember what we said.

Here is a fun experiment.

Write down a list of random words. Try to memorize them. It will be hard to keep them in our long-term memory. But an entire experience, filled with emotion, will be remembered almost forever. Maybe we will remember the first time we cried at school. Or how embarrassed we felt in our first public speech. Or the time we got engaged. Experiences with emotion stay with us longer.

How do we get prospects emotional?

Getting our prospects to switch from autopilot to emotional is something within our control. That's great news. But how is it done?

One great way is by changing the words we use. Certain words are more emotionally charged than others. Here are some random emotional words that advertisers use on us. Do these words stir emotion in us?

Pain	Love
Money	Free
Baby	New
Mother	Secret
Backstabbing	Hooked
Loss	Death

Punish	Wonder
Sinful	Bitter
Obnoxious	Mad
Craving	Snotty
Want	Disgusting
Urge	Bully
Banned	Lies
Smuggled	Coward
Shame	Hate
Hidden	Rage
Confidential	Resent
Cancer	Outrage
Now	Payback
Freedom	Abuse
Travel	Ruthless
Holiday	Losers
Taxes	Dirty
Withheld	Sleazy
Unauthorized	Insider
Home	Security
Arrogant	Unconditional
Revolting	Tested
Smelly	Lifetime
Evil	Refund
Excite	Best-selling
Controversial	Risky

Spark	Worry
Boost	Anxiety
Rally	Terror
Praise	Concern
Recommend	Doubt
Champion	Creepy
Cheerful	Fooled
Ecstatic	Stupid
Overjoyed	Crazy
Spectacular	Horrific
Miracle	Gullible
Breathtaking	Toxic
Victory	Victim
Magic	Catastrophe
Daring	Bloodcurdling
Heartfelt	Trap
Eye-opening	Disaster
Fearless	Collapse
Hero	Mistake
Conquer	Warning
Defy	Embarrass
Heart	Poison
Guts	Nightmare
Perky	

I am sure you can think of more words. However, this is a good list to start with.

Change now!

A slight change of words and our emotions change. Here are some examples of choosing better words.

Instead of child, say "baby."

Instead of house, say "home."

Instead of small human, say "infant." (Yes, engineers have used the words "small human.")

Instead of lose weight, say "victory over fat."

Instead of missed opportunity, say "nightmares of regret."

Instead of bad lab results, say "blood-curdling doctor tests."

Instead of bad boss, say "ruthless boss."

Instead of tastes good, say "sinful taste."

Instead of chemical-based cleaners, say "toxic cleaners."

In these examples, we are adding one emotion-packed word. Think what will happen when we start adding extra emotional words. These emotion-filled statements will spur action and be remembered.

Emotion makes everything better.

The eight-year-old wonderkid was a failure.

When I first started in 1972, one of my first sales leaders was a single mom. With 12 children, she gave home meetings whenever she could. Her eight-year-old daughter came also. She was excited about her mother's future success. In fact, when her mother won a trip to Hawaii, she took her eight-year-old daughter with her.

Children learn fast. Her eight-year-old daughter would stand in front of a room with a marker and an easel, and explain the entire compensation plan.

Impressive? Yes.

Effective? No.

Anyone can memorize product details. And anyone can memorize compensation plans. But that is not why prospects join.

It is our ability to talk to specific programs in their subconscious minds that brings decisions.

In this case, the mother's internal drive and belief oozed out of her every pore. Even as she struggled with the words, people could see her passion and commitment to go all the way to the top. They wanted to go with her.

This was a good start. Her next step was to learn magic words and phrases. This meant her message became more effective. Now, fewer prospects blocked her message. Her results went up. This made her even more attractive as a sponsor.

Every day she looked for new and better ways to deliver her message. And that was the difference between her as a leader, and those that followed her.

Here is an example of an original message, and the improved version.

Original message: "As a mom, you can earn money for your children's private school. Then they can walk from your house."

STRATEGY #5: EMOTION IS OUR PROSPECT'S FRIEND.

Changed message: "As a **mother**, you can earn money for your **babies'** private school now. Then they can walk from your **home**."

Small changes. A few emotional words made the difference. Her sponsoring improved. More neighborhood moms joined.

Selling future benefits is hard.

No one wants to buy life insurance. No one wants to exercise for months to get fit. Humans worry about now.

Humans say, "Tomorrow? Ah, let's not worry about that now."

What can we say to change this? How do we get our prospects to think about the future? Let's try some better messages now by adding a little emotion.

Saving for retirement:

"With our current jobs, it is already too late to save enough for our retirement. We missed our chance by not saving 20% of our salaries when we were 25 years old. That means we either work the rest of our lives until we die ... or start a small part-time business now, so we will have plenty of money when we want to retire."

Utilities:

"Still overpaying on those utility bills? Let's get online now and stop them from overcharging you again next month."

Health:

"Getting older? Yes, it is coming. And there will be a huge gap between the people with great health, enjoying their lives ... and those trapped in the system of doctor appointments, paperwork, and frustration."

Legal services:

"Feel bad when others are not fair? Stop feeling like a victim and claim what is yours. Stop cheaters immediately with an instant phone call to your attorney. Intimidation works."

Nutrition:

"Dying early is inconvenient. Stop aging now before it is too late."

Dieting:

"Turn your body into a fat-burning machine now. Lose weight while you watch television. Make your clothes baggy in only seven days."

Skincare:

"Wrinkles are overrated. They give us character but not much else. Use this wrinkle-shrinking cream so that people stop judging your face."

Opportunity:

"Fire your dream-sucking vampire boss! No more groveling for a raise. Give yourself the income you deserve."

Commuting:

"Escape the life-sucking two-hour daily commutes. Don't become a victim of the rat race."

Education:

"We don't want our children to become day laborers. Let's earn 'private school' bonus checks now."

A bit much? Maybe. But do we feel the emotion? This is the type of emotion that prompts quick decisions. We won't get decisions by leaving behind brochures and links to online videos. We don't want people to get stuck in the information-collecting tar pit.

Sounds good, but can't get the conversation started?

Talking about the future shows we have insights into our prospects' world.

We predict a future problem, and let them know we have a solution. Now our prospects can volunteer to continue the conversation. Use these easy words, "You might be interested" or "Would you like to know?"

Some examples.

Us: "You are going to pay more in taxes in a few years. You might be interested in what we can do to avoid that."

If we were a financial advisor, this would be a non-abrasive, safe statement to make to prospects.

Using this pattern, here are more statements.

"Your body's metabolism will get slower, year by year. You might be interested in how we can avoid that."

"Wrinkles will come faster and faster once we turn 40. You might be interested in how we can delay that."

"Taxes and prices continue to rise, much faster than our salaries. You might be interested in how we can beat that trend."

"Traffic and commuting will get worse. They won't be building any new highways through residential neighborhoods for us. You might be interested in how you can work from home instead."

"Competition is getting fierce, and big salary increases are in the past. You might be interested in how you can give yourself your own salary increases."

As leaders, our job is to create these easy-to-use statements for our team members. When our team sees how rejection-free these statements are, they will use them more often. We want to build habits, and not depend on willpower. Imagine what would happen if our team members used these types of statements several times a day.

More statements using, "Would you like to know how I am doing it?"

"I am making my body younger. Would you like to know how I am doing it?"

"As we get older, we get a lot of inflammation. You probably felt it this morning. I found out how to keep it away. Would you like to know how I am doing it?"

"I am cutting back to four days a week. Would you like to know how I am doing it?"

"I am getting rid of my car payment. Would you like to know how I am doing it?"

"Stopping wrinkles? I found out how. Would you like to know how I am doing it?"

"Identity theft? I don't have to worry about it. Would you like to know how I am doing it?"

"Enough money for retirement? I have it figured out. Would you like to know how I am doing it?"

"Good-paying jobs for young people? Only in our dreams. But I found out how to create those kinds of jobs. Would you like to know how I am doing it?"

Can adding emotion help us with our prospects' procrastination?

Of course. Emotion is an excellent tool to prompt our prospects to make the decision now, instead of in the future.

Have we ever heard this?

Prospect: "I want to think it over."

We think, "Really??? What could our prospect learn later? We already gave all the information."

Now is the best time for our prospect to make the decision. Everything is fresh in his memory.

Then, why does our prospect procrastinate?

Because our prospect is **afraid** to make a decision. Fear is a powerful emotion that tells our prospect what to do.

This is easy to fix.

We can get our prospect's decision now with this mini-story that includes some emotional words. Ready?

"**Imagine** you are standing in the middle of a busy freeway. A huge truck **speeds** towards you. **Scary!** You **wonder** if you should move to the right, or move to the left.

"You **decide** to think about it. **Splat!**

"Life **makes** the decision for you. You **missed** your opportunity to **choose.**

"**Don't let life make the choice** for you. You will **lose** this opportunity to be in **control** of your life.

"Either **choice**, to stay where you are, or to **move** forward is fine. But here is **your chance** to be in **charge** of your **choices.**"

Our prospect realizes there is no delaying the decision. It is either a decision to keep everything as it is and continue this frustrating life, or a decision to move forward with us.

Simple.

By adding a bit of emotion, we can direct our prospect to make the decision now.

Want to see another example of adding a few emotional words to help with an objection?

Objection: "I don't think I should start now. Things are not looking good at my job. I need to conserve my cash."

Us: "I would be **scared** too. You have **all** your eggs in one basket. And your job and boss **control the basket**. That is a **horrible feeling**. You don't look like the sort of person that likes **taking big risks**. Let's start a second income now, so if your job goes away, you won't **lose** 100% of your income."

Could we use a micro-story to help eliminate our prospects' procrastination? Sure. Here is an example.

Us: "My neighbor could have joined the same day I did, but did not. My neighbor will **never be able to forget** that happened.

Every day when he leaves for work, he sees my car parked in the driveway."

Our prospect does not want to be like the neighbor. It will be hard to forget this story.

This is fun. Let's look at one more way to handle procrastination, using some emotional words.

"All the business opportunities you've looked at before tried to **confuse** you with so many tiny details. You got the **feeling** they were **hiding something**. They were. They made it **impossible** for you to see the **big picture**. Here is what you need to know. The **trap** is that you don't know how to do any of these businesses yet. The difference is, we will train you. Now you can get the money you want."

It is fun when we destroy the competition with a few words.

Summary.

Facts, figures, videos, PowerPoint slides, and information put our prospects into analytical mode. Not much decision-making will happen when they are in that mode.

Emotions trigger the decision process.

STRATEGY #6:
HANDLING OBJECTIONS.

Objections happen. They feel less scary when we understand why they occur.

Why do we get objections?

Maybe our prospects don't need what we offer. Possible, but unlikely. We wouldn't be talking to them unless we saw how our products or opportunity could solve their problems.

Our prospects fear change. Very possible. But this is our fault. We know they have this program, and we forgot to position our message with minimal change.

Our prospects fear the unknown future. Of course they want to stay safe where they are, but we failed to make them aware of the dangers of not taking action.

Our prospects don't understand. No one wants to make a decision on what they don't understand. We can help them by using examples, metaphors, similes, and analogies.

Our prospects reacted to us when we said the wrong words. We should prepare our message carefully before visiting with our prospects.

Our prospects don't trust us. Hmmm. This is basic. This should never happen to us as professionals. We never end the rapport step until we have trust and belief from our prospects.

Our prospects don't want to be sold. Many prospects have programs against salespeople. Our strategy should not be to sell them, but to allow them to buy.

Our prospects hold different beliefs and programs. We must reposition our message to be in line with their current beliefs and programs.

Yes, there are many, many reasons for objections. We want to determine the cause of these objections. Then we can form a strategy for our answers.

Prospects are not mean.

Prospects' objections have nothing to do with us personally. They just don't feel comfortable moving forward with what we proposed.

How do we handle this? We make them feel comfortable. We explain things more clearly. We show them facts and viewpoints they didn't know about. We re-frame their objections into a positive view. Yes, we have many tools at our disposal. Let's look at a few.

As we all know, the first rule of objections is to agree.

This keeps communication open. If we disagree, our prospects will be thinking, "Okay, I need to have more ammunition to support my position." While their conscious minds think of more reasons to support their position, they are not listening to us. Remember, the conscious mind can only have one thought at a time.

Let's see some solutions in action.

Objection: "I am not interested."

Us: "You're right. You shouldn't be interested in our business. However, you might be interested in getting an extra check from our business. That could help pay for Heather's school."

Our prospects' subconscious minds activate their love of their children and their curiosity programs. Now our conversation can continue.

Here is another example.

Objection: "I am not interested."

Us: "The last two people I talked to said exactly that. When they found out this was a way for them to work out of their homes instead of commuting, they wanted to know more. Would you like to know what they found out?"

Our prospects' subconscious minds activate their freedom and curiosity programs. Now our conversation can continue.

This is starting to be fun.

Objection: "I am not interested."

Us: "Of course. It is hard to be interested because I failed to tell you how much money you will make. Is it okay if I give you the evidence? Then, it is up to you."

Our prospects' subconscious minds will deactivate their fear of salesmen and fear of change programs. The evidence hook creates curiosity. Now our conversation can continue.

Shall we do another example?

Objection: "I am not interested in changing my electricity."

Us: "I understand. I didn't mean to infer that you would have to change your electricity. I just wanted you to take the online discount. No use paying those extra charges every month."

Our prospects' subconscious minds activate their fear of missing out program. Our conversation can continue.

Objection: "I am not interested. I am too busy already."

Us: "You are the busiest person I know. You have no time to visit. I can help you have more time. Could we talk about it during lunch one day, so it wouldn't take away any of your precious time?"

Our prospects' subconscious minds activate their fear of missing out program. Now our conversation can continue. Or, in some cases, this response could be appropriate.

Objection: "I am not interested. I am too busy already."

Us: "Starting your own part-time business takes time. Time you don't have right now. You are too busy to add more things to your life. While starting a business takes time, it does have some important benefits. Would you like to know why some of your too-busy friends decided to take those benefits?"

Our prospects' curiosity program takes over, and now our conversation can continue. Notice how we did not violate our prospects' beliefs about being too busy? When we stay consistent with their beliefs, we keep communication open.

Objection: "I don't have any money to get started."

Us: "Of course you don't have any money. That is why I am talking to you now. You don't want to be that way for the rest of your life. So let's sit down now, and figure out a way to get you started."

Our prospects have to agree. They don't want to be without money for the rest of their lives. We started with agreement, and then it was easy to transition to the future.

Objection: "I don't have any money to get started."

Us: "That is the first thing I said when I saw this business. And then I thought, 'I've worked all my life, my plan is failing. My friends think I am a failure. I can't keep doing things this way.' Then I figured out how to get the money together to change my life."

Prospects worry about what others think about them. Humans have deep-seated programs to fit in with groups. We changed the objection from money to getting our prospects to think about how others judge them.

What else can we do to help prospects with their objections?

In some cases, a simple reframing or repositioning takes away objections.

We can turn the current objection into a reason to buy or join. How does that work?

Prospects: "I don't think I have the personality to do this business."

Us: "Relax. The good news is that we have dozens of people who were in exactly the same situation when they first started. They learned and became successful and are here to support you. You are in very good company."

Now our prospects can't use this objection because we made the objection a reason they should join.

Another example?

Prospects: "I don't feel confident that this business will work for me."

Us: "Everyone feels that way in the beginning. The good news is that you already know what you are doing now is not working, so there is no harm in giving this business a try."

What about anxiety from a lack of skills? Easy. We could say this:

Prospects: "I don't know that I have the skills needed to make this business work."

Us: "I don't know how far you want to go in your network marketing business. But the good news is that we can choose to learn new skills to go as far as we want."

This repositioning, "learning new skills will make us more successful," removes the objection. Our prospect now sees success as choosing to learn new skills.

When all else fails.

Our prospect folds his arms, frowns, and insists, "I need to think it over."

We take the hint.

When we hear this from a resistant prospect, many times we can use this same prospect's resistance in our favor. How?

By commanding our prospect to think it over.

Huh? Tell our prospect to think it over?

Our prospect is in competitive mode, and wants to resist us. But our prospect can't resist us if we recommend that he thinks it over.

If our prospect thinks it over, that would be agreeing with us. The only way this prospect can resist us is by making a decision now, instead of thinking it over.

How would this sound in real life?

Prospect: "I want to think it over."

Us: "I want you to spend more time, days and weeks, checking out the competition. You should compare tiny details, and put off starting your business. You should only start after you finish collecting information. That way, weeks or months for now, when you are finally ready to start earning money, you will realize that our opportunity and training will be the best choice."

What is our prospect thinking? "I've already spent hours, days, and weeks looking for an opportunity. And now you are telling me to waste even more time doing it? And if I continue investigating, soon everything will look the same. The real key is training, and working with a sponsor who is confident like you. Maybe I should join now. I don't want to put off earning the extra money I need."

Here is another way to answer this resistant prospect.

Prospect: "I want to think it over. I want to research and compare other opportunities."

Us: "Great idea. So many business opportunities try to confuse us with truckloads of tiny details. It is almost impossible to remember the big picture. That is only natural. Here is what you need to know. It will be easy for you to remember this while you evaluate the other businesses. When we choose a business, we don't know how to run that business yet. Our difference is that we will train you. It's comprehensive training that you can complete at your own pace. Now you can get the money you want."

What happens?

We changed the conversation and criteria in our prospect's head. Now our competition's hype and details will have less effect. Our prospect thinks, "I should make a business decision based upon comprehensive training. And, you're already offering that to me now."

This approach will not work for green personalities. Green personalities love collecting information. But for the other three personality types, this could redirect the decision away from checking out the competition. Now the decision will be made based on comprehensive training.

And finally, if we have no idea what is holding our prospects back, we can ask them.

However, it appears aggressive when we ask, "What is holding you back?"

We can do better than that. Let's try this.

Us: "I know you love the idea of our business, but nothing is perfect. What concerns you most at the moment?"

Our prospects will feel more comfortable answering this question. Their answer helps us limit their decision to just one thing. If there is more than one thing holding them back, now is a great time for us to find this out.

Change the decision to something else.

When prospects fixate on something we cannot change, turn the discussion to something else. Two quick examples.

Prospects: "But I would rather order something similar online. It would be cheaper than your health products."

Us: "Your online contact will be a minimum-wage customer service representative. You will probably get a different person every time you call. But this is your health we're talking about. I will be your health coach every time you call. This is your health and your life. You don't want to mess this up."

Prospects: "I can't justify paying that kind of money for a water filter."

Us: "This isn't something that we justify like buying a dishwasher, or a $1,000 smartphone. This is something we do for our health and our life. Can you imagine how we will feel when we are healthy and strong while our fellow retirees suffer poor health and massive drug bills?"

Still running into the cost objection? We can compare the price with something already familiar in our prospects' minds.

Prospects: "I don't want to pay that much for a water filter."

Us: "Yes, this alkaline water filter is expensive, **but** it won't cost you anything. It is the same price you will pay for bottled water over the next few years. You will pay for this water filter whether you get it or not, so why not get it?"

STRATEGY #7:
USE ANALOGIES, SIMILES, METAPHORS AND EXAMPLES.

How can we help our prospects understand our messages better? By using analogies, similes, metaphors and examples. Our prospects connect our new information to something they already understand. This means our prospects don't have to create a network of new neural pathways for our message. Our brains appreciate the easier route.

Why does this work so well? Our new message is easier for our prospects to process because they can associate it with something already in their minds. They only have to encode and process the differences in our new information.

Objections from our prospects can be a sign that they don't understand what we understand. Instead of dumping facts and information, we will make comparisons with something they already know. This shortens their learning curve.

Take a look at the following objections. We explain our answer by comparing our new information with something our prospects feel familiar with.

Prospect: "Why is your food supplement so expensive?"

Us: "Think about an apple tree. Only a small portion of the apple tree is edible and good for us, the apple. But, if we wanted to make it cheaper, we could grind up the roots, the bark, the branches, and the leaves. Then put that powder into capsules. Yes, it would be 'apple,' but it wouldn't help your health. We wouldn't compromise your health just to make more profit."

Now, what will our prospects be thinking about when they see a cheaper version of our product? They will have doubts about the quality and the performance of our competitors.

Prospect: "Why is your food supplement so expensive?"

Us: "Your health is like taking a trip to work on the freeway. You can choose to buy a car. Or to save money, you could choose to buy a bicycle for your trip on the busy freeway. Which would you like to risk your health on?"

The answer to this is obvious. Our prospects understand the difference between a bicycle and a car for safety. By using this comparison, we make it easy for our prospects' brains to relate to our new information.

More examples?

Prospect: "Your skincare program is expensive."

Us: "Taking good care of your skin requires constant vigilance. Now, you can save money by having an 11-year-old babysitter, or be safe with a professional nanny in charge of your precious baby. We are like the professional nanny, guaranteeing great results with your skin before it is too late."

Prospect: "This business opportunity seems overwhelming. There are too many things to learn and do."

Us: "That is a common feeling. However, it is just like driving a car. During the first days of driving, we struggle to keep the car in the middle of the road. Later, we add new skills. And two months later? We drive down the road on autopilot, not even giving a thought to the multiple things we are doing. You will have the same experience here."

We want to relate our message to something familiar, something our prospects already know. Now it is easy for their brains to grasp our message.

STRATEGY #8: PATTERNS BECOME SMOOTH PATHWAYS FOR OUR PROSPECTS' MINDS.

Think of children. At birth, their brains are only partially developed. It will take years for their brains to learn how to survive in an adult's world.

What are they looking for during this time? How to function in this world.

How do they learn? By looking for patterns. Is this familiar?

The child screams, the parents pick up and comfort the child. The child notices the pattern, and repeats it. Sometimes it takes longer to train the parents, but eventually the child knows, "If I scream, my parents will pick me up and try to make me happy."

The child will use this pattern over and over again.

The child wants sugar. Scream, and the odds of getting sugar go way up. Screaming at parents while grocery shopping gets fast results. Parents don't want the public embarrassment.

Screaming at home for sugar doesn't work as well. There isn't enough social pressure for the parents to give in. No one is watching.

Asking for sugar with the words, "Would it be okay if," gets better results than other word sequences.

Asking for sugar after 6PM when the parents are tired will get better results.

Doing a good deed, and then asking for sugar, manipulates the parents to be more open-minded about a sugar reward.

Children survive by looking for patterns. That is how they learn.

Fortunately, we retain our fascination with patterns. We look for meaning in things in our lives. Why did this event happen? Why did someone get angry? What caused this? Is there a pattern?

Once we have a pattern, it is easy to repeat. We don't have to build new neural pathways. We have those neural pathways already. It seems natural. No thinking involved.

Do our prospects have patterns? Of course.

If we follow a pattern that our prospects feel is natural, our chances of success increase.

How do we know what patterns our prospects like?

Ask.

This works best for products or services. What we offer could be replacing a product or service our prospects have now.

Pattern-matching doesn't work as well for a business opportunity. Most prospects don't have a pattern for joining business opportunities. Maybe they've never joined one before. Or maybe they joined one because their brother-in-law came to the house. This is harder to duplicate.

Of course, if someone has joined multiple opportunities before, they will have a pattern. Just ask.

Let's take a look at a few examples of patterns used for purchasing products. Here are the questions we could ask. The answers will tell us exactly which pattern our prospects will use to buy from us.

Diet products.

Us: "Have you ever gone on a diet before?"

Prospect: "Yes. If there is a diet, I've tried it." (Our prospect is telling us he will try any **new** diet. It doesn't get any easier than this.)

Us: "This diet is brand-new. You are going to love it."

Here is another conversation. This time we will see a negative pattern we will avoid.

Us: "Have you ever dieted before?"

Prospect: "Yes. I tried a low-carbohydrate diet. I ended up craving bread and pasta so much that as soon as I stopped my diet, all my weight came back."

Us: "That is normal. No one wants to suffer with cravings and give up their favorite foods. We need to have a diet that fits our lifestyle."

Now, what is our prospect thinking? "If you have a different diet that includes carbohydrates, I am ready."

Patterns are not difficult to pick up from our prospects.

Us: "How did you choose your current cellphone carrier?"

Prospect: "I saw an ad in the mail. It promised to lower my monthly rate."

Us: "Arranging for a lower rate make sense. We can use the money on other things in our lives."

What is our prospect thinking? "If you have a lower rate, I should switch immediately."

One more example.

Us: "How did you choose your current annual holiday?"

Prospect: "First, I check how much money I have. Then, I go online and try to find a good deal. I want to save money."

Us: "Our travel program has access to all the online deals, plus hidden packages that only travel agents know about. Let's see how far you can go with your budget now, and prepare to be surprised with the savings."

We love our habits. We love familiar patterns.

When we keep our prospects' patterns in mind, they don't have to do a lot of mental work to understand what we offer. We go down the same familiar neural pathways.

Strategy #9:
Our biased prospects only hear part of what we say.

Relax. This is normal. Everyone has biases. These beliefs and programs give us our points of view. Here is an example.

Two teams play a game. The winning team's fans believe the game was awesome. The losing team's fans see the outcome quite differently.

Same game. Two different viewpoints.

Our internal biases tell us what to think and believe about neutral facts and events. As professional network marketers, we should be aware of our prospects' biases.

One of the most common biases? The confirmation bias.

The confirmation bias tells us that what we currently believe is true, and:

1. We reject or discount anything that contradicts our beliefs.

2. We pay attention to and love anything that is in line with our beliefs.

That is why when two people see the same information, they can come away with completely different views. Think of a political speech. If we are a member of that politician's political party, their message resonates and we believe everything they say.

If we are not a member of that political party, we interpret that same information as a reason not to believe that person.

In short, our biases tell us how to interpret new information.

Our biases also interfere with our brains. We must be aware of biases when we design our conversations with our prospects. Here are two quick examples of prospects with biases, and how we can customize our presentation to complement their biases.

Example #1. Selling our business opportunity.

Our prospect believes financial security for the family is important. The steady and dependable feeling that comes from a paycheck means security. Our prospect sees risk as dangerous.

Showing our opportunity as a chance to be independent? That's not going to agree with his bias.

But, why not present our part-time income as a way to **reduce** the risk of having all of one's income from one source? Now our prospect's bias toward security is working for us, instead of against us.

When we know our prospects' biases, we can present our message in a favorable light.

Example #2. Selling diet products.

Overweight people didn't become overweight from strenuous exercise. To avoid exercise they use excuses such as:

- "I am too tired when I get home from work."
- "My knees hurt when I walk around."
- "Exercise takes up too much time away from my family."
- "Exercise is hard. That's for young people."

Show them an exercise video, and already they are looking for reasons why exercise will not work for them. Offer them a gym membership, and they might have a heart attack.

But what viewpoints or biases do these overweight people have? Let's list a few.

- "It is hard to diet when I am hungry."
- "I love the taste of food."
- "I can't go to bed on an empty stomach."
- "Being hungry all the time makes me irritable."

So, our message will be:

"Going hungry slows down your metabolism. You need to eat food. Start your morning with this delicious chocolate power shake to tingle your taste buds, fix your craving for chocolate, and to give your fat-burning metabolism a boost."

Now we are in line with our prospects' biases.

How do we figure out our prospects' biases?

Empathy.

Understanding our prospects' biases is easy when we have empathy.

Empathy means we understand and share our prospects' feelings. We try to see things from their points of view. Take a few seconds before we start. Observe our prospects and their surroundings. They may have hard-core biases that will sabotage our message.

An example?

My best friend was a nerdy chemical engineer. As an analytical personality, he accumulated all the "correct" research, then tortured the data until the research said what he wanted it to say. For nutrition products, he would read labels and source out the lowest-priced suppliers of each ingredient.

The result of all of his investigation? He never bought a single nutritional product. He was stuck in permanent research mode.

Understanding his bias on price, I knew this was a no-win situation. So what was the new strategy?

I used examples of what he was familiar with. The conversation went like this.

Me: "Tell me about your car."

Prospect: "This car has the highest ratings for performance. I use premium gasoline only to make sure it holds its high resale value. I enjoy the smooth ride and acceleration when I need it."

Me: "Did you see that new car on television that is half the price? It gets a lot of advertising."

Prospect: "That car is a cheap piece of junk. I wouldn't risk my life on that tinfoil death-trap."

Me: "That is a great phone you have."

Prospect: "Not a great phone, the best phone. It can do everything I want, and doesn't slow down like my old phone. It sets the standard for performance, and is rated the best phone on the market."

Me: "Why not get a cheaper phone? With the money you save, you can upgrade your lunches to jumbo french fries for a month."

Prospect: "Cheap phones are cheap. They break down. They lock up. That is why I got this model. It works!"

Me: "It is good that you take care of yourself. You value what is important. These vitamins have everything you need, so you don't have to buy from 35 different places. Your time is worth a little more than a few dollars. And your body is worth taking care of."

Prospect: "Yeah, that does make some sense. I am worth every penny."

When we know our prospects' biases, it is easy to position our products or opportunity to be in line with how they see the world.

Remember, we talk, but our prospects will reject much of what we say because of their biases. Then, they will forget most of the remaining message.

What is left? Only a little.

We want to make sure we focus on making that little bit of remaining message strong.

Humans can only remember a tiny percentage of what they experience. We want to be part of that tiny percentage.

STRATEGY #10:
STORIES ARE IRRESISTIBLE.

Tony Miehle sells insurance, and he does it well. What separates Tony from other insurance salesmen? His ability to tell stories.

Tony knows his job is to get people to insure themselves and their families. But to get the decision, Tony doesn't recite facts, figures, amortization data, and life expectancy charts. Most prospects don't understand those things. It is unfair to ask them to make decisions on what they don't understand. That is why they asked Tony to talk to them. Insurance can be complicated.

Then what does Tony present? A story. He knows this is an easier way to communicate complicated new information. He keeps a collection of appropriate short stories to illustrate and explain how insurance can help. Here is an example.

"Insurance is all about risk. If you get into a car crash, your car insurance repairs your car. If your home burns down, your homeowner's insurance rebuilds your house. And if you die, your life insurance brings you back to life, right? (Chuckle.) Obviously not. The purpose of life insurance is to make sure your family isn't financially devastated while they are emotionally devastated. It is really a love letter you leave behind for your family."

The secret ingredient to his success is telling short, easy-to-understand stories. Then he allows his prospects to decide if they want life insurance or not. If they do want to buy, only then will Tony explain the details they might want to know.

So why do stories work so well?

Cavemen squatted around the fire telling stories. One would say, "If you see a giant lizard out there, that is called a dinosaur. It will eat you. Don't play with them." (Okay, cavemen came much later than the dinosaurs, but this story is easier to remember.)

The cavemen that listened said, "Wow. What a great story. Now we don't have to experience this in person. This will help us survive."

Then the smarter cavemen formed a program in their minds: "If anyone tells us a story, we have to listen. That story could be important to our future survival."

What happened to the cavemen that didn't form a program to listen to stories? Well, they became predator food. They did not reproduce. All the descendants from the smarter cavemen have a program that says, "If anyone tells us a story, we have to listen. That story could be important to our future survival."

When we walk past a group, and someone is telling a story, our subconscious mind commands us to stop and listen. We love stories. That is why we like books, movies, gossip, and more. As soon as they can talk, children will plead with their parents, "Mommy, Daddy, please tell me a story."

How does this apply to our prospects and their decisions?

Stories are the natural way for our prospects to learn.

This makes learning effortless for them. Cavemen did not have PowerPoint and videos. They didn't even have brochures!

STRATEGY #10: STORIES ARE IRRESISTIBLE.

Memorizing facts, figures, and information is difficult. When our prospects hear a story, their minds understand the story and the story's consequences. It is part of our DNA.

Want our prospects to remember us and our message? Tell a story. Stories are naturally easy to remember. Stories hold our attention. We can't remember a grocery list one day after we make it. But stories? We can remember the entire plot of a movie we saw years ago.

But this all gets better.

Prospects feel less skepticism about the facts of a story. Stories are familiar and feel safe for them to listen to. With less skepticism, our prospects relax, and our rapport improves. Our prospects love doing business with people they like.

And are stories pleasant for our minds? Yes. Boring fact-filled lectures are painful to our minds. But stories? We love stories.

There are lots of reasons to use stories to get our prospects to make decisions. But here is our favorite reason to use stories.

We think in facts. We feel stories!

Minds feel stories. They experience the emotions. They see imagined scenes. They feel like the stories are happening to them.

What does this mean for our message? Any time we can put our message into a story, we multiply the effect of our story with prospects. If possible, avoid facts, data, and boring information. Emotions are the key to making lasting memories.

We want to become "story machines."

Here is a good rule: **"When in doubt, tell a story."**

Some people are natural storytellers. Others have to re-learn the structure of a story step-by-step. But most of us have been telling stories all our lives. All we need are a few **prompts**. We can take it from there.

The words, "Once upon a time," announce that we are about to tell a children's story. We need similar opening words to announce that we will be telling our prospects a business story.

Here are some opening prompts and short examples:

"Suppose that ..."

"Suppose that your teenage daughter comes to you one morning. She cries, 'My acne is getting worse! I don't want to go to school. I am ashamed of these pimples!' You understand how fragile your daughter's self-image is during these high school years and you want to help. You call me to get a good skincare system to improve your daughter's complexion. So that is what I do. I turn skin problems into happy customers."

"The boss said he had bad news."

"The boss announced to our office that he had some bad news. He said, 'Business is bad. Half of you will have to take a 40% pay cut. The other half, we will terminate your jobs in 60 days.'

"One employee asked, 'So what is our option if we don't like these two choices?'

"The boss answered, 'Oh, if you don't like those two choices, I have some good news. You are fired immediately, and have the rest of the afternoon off.'

"And because of that experience, I will never let 100% of my income come from one job. I will always have a part-time business on the side for security."

"I looked at my bank account and saw …"

"I looked at my bank account and immediately a flush came to my face. My normally overdrawn account had over $3,000! That was the highest bank balance of my life. This month's bonus check was more than I expected. This part-time business changed my life."

"It was Black Friday."

"It was Black Friday. The day's buying frenzy would put thousands extra into my bank account. The best decision I ever made was to start this part-time business nine months ago."

"My doctor was furious!"

"My doctor was furious! I stopped accepting new medications every visit, and decided to make a change in my life. Instead of mindlessly accepting generic medical advice that masked my symptoms, I decided to take charge of my health. I stopped eating junk food, started exercising, and took lots of supplements. I wanted to give my body the best chance to get well. And it worked. My health is back to normal and I said good-bye to the monthly doctor visits. I hope he can make his swimming pool payments without my business."

"When my banker turned me down."

"When my banker turned me down, I had to take an honest look at my life. After working for 20 years, I wasn't even worthy of a $5,000 personal loan. Ouch.

"It appears that I worked 20 years for the auto finance, the mortgage, the credit cards, and the utility bills. And out of 20 years of hard work, there was nothing for me. I knew it was time to get serious about my finances."

"Here is the short story."

"Here is the short story. I hated bills. Just the thought of opening those envelopes stressed me out. High cellphone bills, but my family needs cellphones. High electricity bills that kept going up and up, but no one can live without electricity. The first thing I did was go online to get discounts on my bills. Next, I told 15 other people to do the same. Now, my bills are free. I smile every time they show up in the mail."

"I will never forget the day ..."

"I will never forget the day I found out my neighbor paid less on his cellphone bill, and we had the exact same service! It felt like a knife in the back when he told me he knew how to get lower rates, and he didn't even tell me. Some neighbors can't pass the 'friend test.'"

And then what happens?

Most prospects see themselves in our stories. They feel the emotions we felt. And these emotions trigger a decision in prospects: "Yes, this is something I should do."

And our prospects love this. Why? These short stories help them understand and feel our message. Now they can make an immediate decision, "Do I want this or not?"

We can't go wrong if we think, "Stories first." If we feel that our stories won't be interesting, there is an easy solution. Pick a story that our prospects can't resist. And what story would that be?

A story of a personal failure.

Prospects love hearing about our failures. It's irresistible. Humans learn from other people's failures. And, other people's failures make them feel superior. Everyone loves a feeling of superiority. If we can't think of any stories for our business, try this. We can tell of the failure or failures we had that prompted us to start our new network marketing business. Here are two short examples.

"I thought having a regular business would be great."

"I thought having a regular business would be great. Unfortunately, I forgot about unmotivated employees. Employees that don't show up for work. Employees that are rude to customers. And even employees that 'borrow' things from work and never bring them back. No matter how much I sold, I still had to pay my employees. The day I sold my store was the happiest day of my life. And when I started my network marketing business, what was the best news? No employees. No more stress for me. I could build a business without worry."

"I got ripped off at work."

"I got ripped off at work. At the beginning of the year, the boss promised big bonuses if we had a successful year. We worked hard, made a profit, and the boss changed his mind. I had all my eggs in one basket, my job. I will never make that mistake again. That is why I am doing this part-time business, so I will have some security in my life."

Stories are human.

We are in the person-to-person business. If we want the message from our brains to enter the brains of our prospects, stories are the answer. We might notice that the top leaders in network marketing are great storytellers. We should remember that.

AND FINALLY ...

Unless we talk clearly to our prospects' brains, we will have terrible results. Our prospects won't take advantage of our wonderful products and services, and they won't take advantage of our opportunity. In some cases, our communication is so bad, our message may never even enter their brains. This is effectively withholding our message from them.

Using these 10 strategies to communicate with our prospects' brains more effectively will help deliver our messages. We are in the decision-making business. Our companies pay us to get "yes" decisions from our prospects. We should take this seriously.

Good luck on using these 10 strategies to deliver your messages.

Thank you.

Thank you for purchasing and reading this book. We hope you found some ideas that will work for you.

Before you go, would it be okay if we asked a small favor? Would you take just one minute and leave a sentence or two reviewing this book online? Your review can help others choose what they will read next. It would be greatly appreciated by many fellow readers.

I travel the world 240+ days each year.
Let me know if you want me to stop in your
area and conduct a live Big Al training.

BigAlSeminars.com

FREE Big Al Training Audios
Magic Words for Prospecting
plus Free eBook and the Big Al Report!

BigAlBooks.com/free

MORE BIG AL BOOKS

How to Get Your Prospect's Attention and Keep It!
Magic Phrases for Network Marketing

Getting attention is the easy part. Keeping that attention requires using these magic phrases to ward off distractions.

Mini-Scripts for the Four Color Personalities
How to Talk to our Network Marketing Prospects

As network marketing leaders, we want to move people to take positive actions. Using their own color language is how we will do it.

Quick Start Guide for Network Marketing
Get Started FAST, Rejection-FREE!

Our new team members are at the peak of their enthusiasm now. Let's give them the fast-start skills to kick-start their business immediately.

The Two-Minute Story for Network Marketing
Create the Big-Picture Story That Sticks!

Worried about presenting your business opportunity to prospects? Here is the solution. The two-minute story is the ultimate presentation to network marketing prospects.

How to Build Your Network Marketing Business in 15 Minutes a Day

Anyone can set aside 15 minutes a day to start building their financial freedom. Of course we would like to have more time, but in just 15 minutes we can change our lives forever.

How to Meet New People Guidebook
Overcome Fear and Connect Now

Meeting new people is easy when we can read their minds. Discover how strangers automatically size us up in seconds, using three basic standards.

How To Get Kids To Say Yes!
Using the Secret Four Color Languages to Get Kids to Listen

Turn discipline and frustration into instant cooperation. Kids love to say "yes" when they hear their own color-coded language.

Why Are My Goals Not Working?
Color Personalities for Network Marketing Success

Setting goals that work for us is easy when we have guidelines and a checklist.

Closing for Network Marketing
Getting Prospects Across The Finish Line

Here are 46 years' worth of our best closes. All of these closes are kind and comfortable for prospects, and rejection-free for us.

Pre-Closing for Network Marketing
"Yes" Decisions Before The Presentation

Instead of selling to customers with facts, features and benefits, let's talk to prospects in a way they like. We can now get that "yes" decision first, so the rest of our presentation will be easy.

The One-Minute Presentation
Explain Your Network Marketing Business Like A Pro

Learn to make your business grow with this efficient, focused business presentation technique.

Retail Sales for Network Marketers
How to Get New Customers for Your MLM Business

Learn how to position your retail sales so people are happy to buy. Don't know where to find customers for your products and services? Learn how to market to people who want what you offer.

Getting "Yes" Decisions
What insurance agents and financial advisors can say to clients

In the new world of instant decisions, we need to master the words and phrases to successfully move our potential clients to lifelong clients. Easy … when we can read their minds and service their needs immediately.

3 Easy Habits For Network Marketing
Automate Your MLM Success

Use these habits to create a powerful stream of activity in your network marketing business.

Start SuperNetworking!
5 Simple Steps to Creating Your Own Personal Networking Group

Start your own personal networking group and have new, pre-sold customers and prospects come to you.

The Four Color Personalities for MLM
The Secret Language for Network Marketing

Learn the skill to quickly recognize the four personalities and how to use magic words to translate your message.

Ice Breakers!
How To Get Any Prospect To Beg You For A Presentation

Create unlimited Ice Breakers on-demand. Your distributors will no longer be afraid of prospecting, instead, they will love prospecting.

How To Get Instant Trust, Belief, Influence and Rapport!
13 Ways To Create Open Minds By Talking To The Subconscious Mind

Learn how the pros get instant rapport and cooperation with even the coldest prospects. The #1 skill every new distributor needs.

First Sentences for Network Marketing
How To Quickly Get Prospects On Your Side

Attract more prospects and give more presentations with great first sentences that work.

Motivation. Action. Results.
How Network Marketing Leaders Move Their Teams

Learn the motivational values and triggers our team members have, and learn to use them wisely. By balancing internal motivation and external motivation methods, we can be more effective motivators.

How To Build Network Marketing Leaders
Volume One: Step-By-Step Creation Of MLM Professionals

This book will give you the step-by-step activities to actually create leaders.

How To Build Network Marketing Leaders
Volume Two: Activities And Lessons For MLM Leaders

You will find many ways to change people's viewpoints, to change their beliefs, and to reprogram their actions.

The Complete Three-Book Network Marketing Leadership Series

Series includes: How To Build Network Marketing Leaders Volume One, How To Build Network Marketing Leaders Volume Two, and Motivation. Action. Results.

51 Ways and Places to Sponsor New Distributors
Discover Hot Prospects For Your Network Marketing Business

Learn the best places to find motivated people to build your team and your customer base.

How To Prospect, Sell And Build Your
Network Marketing Business With Stories

If you want to communicate effectively, add
your stories to deliver your message.

26 Instant Marketing Ideas To Build
Your Network Marketing Business

176 pages of amazing marketing lessons and
case studies to get more prospects for your business
immediately.

Big Al's MLM Sponsoring Magic

How To Build A Network Marketing Team Quickly

This book shows the beginner exactly what to do, exactly
what to say, and does it through the eyes of a brand-new
distributor.

Public Speaking Magic

Success and Confidence in the First 20 Seconds

By using any of the three major openings in this book,
we can confidently start our speeches and presentations
without fear.

Worthless Sponsor Jokes

Network Marketing Humor

Here is a collection of worthless sponsor jokes from 25
years of the "Big Al Report." Network marketing can be
enjoyable, and we can have fun making jokes along
the way.

BigAlBooks.com

ABOUT THE AUTHORS

Keith Schreiter has 20+ years of experience in network marketing and MLM. He shows network marketers how to use simple systems to build a stable and growing business.

So, do you need more prospects? Do you need your prospects to commit instead of stalling? Want to know how to engage and keep your group active? If these are the types of skills you would like to master, you will enjoy his "how-to" style.

Keith speaks and trains in the U.S., Canada, and Europe.

Tom "Big Al" Schreiter has 40+ years of experience in network marketing and MLM. As the author of the original "Big Al" training books in the late '70s, he has continued to speak in over 80 countries on using the exact words and phrases to get prospects to open up their minds and say "YES."

His passion is marketing ideas, marketing campaigns, and how to speak to the subconscious mind in simplified, practical ways. He is always looking for case studies of incredible marketing campaigns that give usable lessons.

As the author of numerous audio trainings, Tom is a favorite speaker at company conventions and regional events.

Made in the USA
Coppell, TX
19 December 2022

90134549R00075